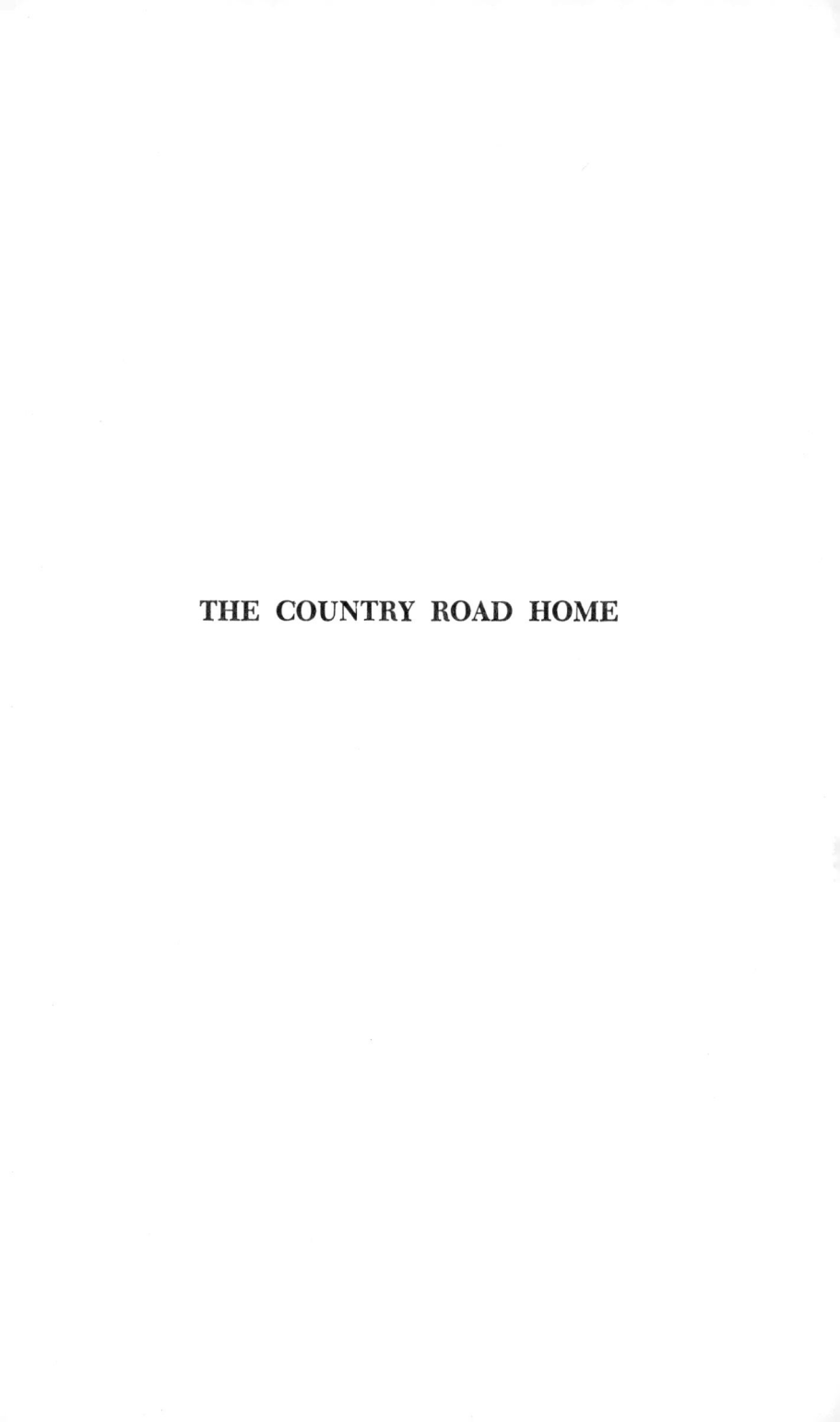

THE COUNTRY ROAD HOME

The Country Road Home

The Story of St. John Vianney
the Curé of Ars

Written and Illustrated
by the
Daughters of St. Paul

ST. PAUL EDITIONS

ISBN 0-8198-0232-8 cloth
      0-8198-1412-1 paper

Library of Congress Catalog Card Number: 66-29166

NIHIL OBSTAT:
   Rt. Rev. John G. Hogan
   Diocesan Censor
IMPRIMATUR:
   ✝ Richard Cardinal Cushing

Copyright © 1987, 1966 by the Daughters of St. Paul

Printed in the U.S.A., by the Daughters of St. Paul
50 St. Paul's Ave., Boston, MA 02130

The Daughters of St. Paul are an international congregation of women religious serving the Church with the communications media.

CONTENTS

PART I

Setting for Saint-Breeding 13

His Goal a Mirage? 18

Just Another Setback 23

The Deserter 27

Ahead...Always Ahead 30

The Backbone of Someone Else 34

Death of a Friend 38

PART II

Pastor of What? 45

One Man Attack 48

The Petition 53

Mates — Curé and the Devil 60

Ars Grows 63

Chamber of Mercy 67

Looking in — or through — a Soul 72

A Monk at Heart 74

The Eternal Pilgrimage 79

PART I

*Of all great hearts, the greatest
is still the heart of a saint. For it wants
to contain not only its neighbor, strangers,
all suffering, sinful, warring humanity—
but God Himself.*

HENRI GHÉON

Chapter 1

SETTING FOR SAINT-BREEDING

A man does not just emerge on the world's scene like a great ice glacier. Nor can he be described that way. Unless he is viewed against the backdrop of the times in which he lived, he becomes just like that glacier, frigid and isolated from the sometimes beautiful, sometimes harsh shore of reality. This holds true when one writes the life of a saint, any saint, even if he be just a peasant priest from the country town of Ars.

The 18th century French climate was like a pressure-cooker near the exploding point. No sooner had John Vianney been born, than the French Revolution began. The Church was persecuted in that age, as in every age. "Constitutional priests" were placed at the head of each parish and so, devout Catholics had to sneak into damp cellars, risking prison, to assist at the Mass of a fugitive loyal priest.

Matthew and Marie Vianney were only country peasants from an equally countrified town called Dardilly. They never did learn to read or write very well, but they knew how to manage their poor farm and make it produce for their six children. They also knew what was the *true* faith and what was not. A family library was out of the question for them, but they did have a Bible. And they read a little of it everyday. They talked about it and they explained it to their children.

However, the Bible was not the only source of grace. The Mass and Sacraments were needed too. Matthew and Marie carted the children with them into dank dungeons or wherever else Mass was being said. They were fools, you might say. But life was not a game of chance with them—it was a matter of Faith. For the great Book, the Bible, said clearly,

"If you believe ... all things are possible to him who believes."

✢

Little John learned many things during those first years. He was very alert and followed quite willingly at his father's heels. He watched the growth of new crops and the harvesting of ripe ones. He learned how to herd sheep at an age when today's youngsters would be going to kindergarten. This life was natural for a peasant lad from the country. But it was not all. He learned about God too, and the parables of the Gospels; the way his father told them impressed the little fellow.

*

To say that John Vianney was born a little saint and then one day grew into a large saint, just would not be the right story. He was human, pleasantly so. He liked to laugh; he liked the companionship of his little friends; he liked the attention of his family; he liked to take walks and play games. Yes, and he liked to win the games too.

But while he was human, the remarkable and wonderful fact of it all is that John Vianney, throughout his whole life, never committed a mortal sin, never even witnessed the committing of a mortal sin. The closest he ever came to one was to forgive the offense in the quietness of his confessional. And this is the truth. It happened in no other way.

The life of a French peasant boy may seem boring to you. But John knew no other. The flaming, surging effects of the Revolution were mere ripples in the life of the lad. The voices of men who screamed that there was no God, that God was dead, faded into obscurity long before their poisonous errors ever infiltrated the tart, clear air of the French countryside. And so he grew up, tending sheep for his dad, attending Mass in secret, receiving his First Communion at the age of 13 in the quiet splendor of a clammy shed. All of these events were planned, planned in the Providence of God, for the molding of a priest, who would one day burst the bonds of Dardilly and Ars, to fill the whole world with the example of his incredible life.

When John was 15, the churches were again opened.

He received his First Communion in the quiet splendor of a clammy shed.

Chapter 2

HIS GOAL A MIRAGE?

For a long time now he had been thinking, weighing, and had finally reached a decision. John went up to his dad on a day which seemed, well, just like any other day, and out of what seemed to be a clear blue sky, made a startling request:

"I want to become a priest."

The old man accepted the request almost with sorrow. He could not afford the education involved. After all, he had five other children to think about. And too, he counted on John and really needed his work on the farm. After a good deal of thought, he had to reply "no."

But day after day that decision haunted Matthew Vianney.

"If he has a vocation, it is God who gave it," he would catch himself thinking. "If it is God's will, then He will provide for my children and my farm."

The tired eyes of his wife pleaded for her boy, yet she withheld her opinion. Matthew was the head of the family.

John plunged deeper into the care of the farm, not forgetting his priestly goal by any means, but willing to wait for God's good time.

And God's good time was fast approaching for Matthew Vianney at last decided, that the expense of tuition and the extra labor of the farm, was not half so burdensome as the battle that was raging within his own conscience.

❊

And so John was off for the "Presbytery School" at Ecully, a neighboring village. The unusually tall, lanky lad, with straight hair almost reaching his eyebrows, presented himself to the rector of the school. He did not make a very impressionable sight.

"I am Father Balley," the kindly, middle-aged rector said, extending his hand.

"And I am John Vianney," the boy said, his thin cheeks flushing violently. "I want to become a priest, you know."

"Yes, that is what your pastor has told me," assured Father Balley. "I want you to become one too."

And so, John Vianney launched his great quest for the priesthood. The work was hard, slow, and progress was equally hard and equally slow. But Father Balley was always near, taking the role of a cheerful guardian angel, tugging and pushing his pupil.

It wasn't that the boy from Dardilly was dumb, but to someone with no formal education, who could barely read or write, to endeavor the study of Latin took courage and faith... a lot more faith than John had. It was Father Balley's faith that saw him through the first slow and painful year of Seminary preparation. By the time summer came, the boy no longer could hide his feelings. He was discouraged.

"I should quit," he confided flatly to Father Balley.

"Over a little bit of Latin," the kindly priest laughed. "I have an idea," he said confidentially to John. "You have a great love for St. John Regis, the patron of your town. Why not make a summer pilgrimage to his shrine? Ask him, son, ask him to make your studies easier. And then return here to continue."

It was worth a try. At this point, anything was worth a try.

Barefoot and without food, John trudged to the town of La Louvesc. Bearing the heat,

For one who could barely read or write, to endeavor the study of Latin took courage and faith.

begging for shelter, he gladly endured the sixty mile trek until the shrine came into view. There, in a place dedicated to a man who had become the greatest of a success—a saint—the boy knelt and mumbled his story. Tears, which had welled for weeks and months, slid steadily down colorless cheeks. And then, his soul felt peace, his burden lighter. John went back to school, back to Father Balley, ready to resume his work. The studies would be no easier, but the discouragement was gone.

In 1807, he was confirmed and took the name "Baptist."

Chapter 3

JUST ANOTHER SETBACK

It could have happened to anybody—but rarely would it. Just when his studies were getting to the bearable stage, another setback introduced itself. The Emperor's war with Spain was dragging on and as someone remarked, he was "drafting everything with two legs." John Vianney, unfortunately, only had two legs. Since he was a seminarian, he was exempt from the draft, but somehow his name was not on the exemption list and so his date for entry was fast approaching. Father Balley went to the War Office to explain the error, but they not only were not interested, they likewise would not change the draft. Father Balley pleaded, coaxed, insisted, in proper turn one after the other. None of his efforts, however, moved so much as one hair on one head of the stuffy personnel. Even after much prayer, when the good priest returned again, the answer was still a definite "no." Could this miserable situation possibly be God's will? Yes, it must be God's will.

*

Dressed in his baggy uniform, John not only looked resigned, he even appeared almost interested. The man who would one day weep for the sins spoken by the nameless voices in the confessional, could take this rather hard knock to his personal life without batting an eyelash. Father Balley shook his hand warmly and then, slapping him on the shoulder, said, "Come back soon, son."

John reported to the headquarters at Lyons. There he fell ill. But recovering soon, he followed his regiment and caught up in Roanne. However, the recovery had not been complete enough. So the would-be soldier was admitted to the hospital.

Soon back on his feet, yet quite a bit wobbly, the boy from Dardilly was assigned to a contingent which was leaving immediately for Spain. While the men were lining up outside, John took the opportunity to drop into the little church, not more than twenty yards away. He set his rifle and knapsack down and was lost in the sparkling freshness of person-to-person communication with the Master.

When it came to practical things, John was a little dense at times. And this, frankly,

"They're gone," he stammered nervously.

was to be one of those times. He emerged from the church—how much later no one knows. But his eyes grew wide in sheer surprise, for the road was empty, and the dust had long since settled.

"They're gone," he stammered nervously. His heart began thumping loud and fast. "They've left me behind," he mumbled over and over.

The tongue lashing received at the barracks was brutal to a sensitive lad like John. He was told, point blank, to catch up to his regiment—fast, or else. The hours were passing, and the confused lad was still not catching up. He began to fear that somewhere along the line, a wrong road had been taken... and he was tired, very tired.

Chapter 4

THE DESERTER

He was resting—just for a while—under a shady tree. The heat of the day had subsided now; the marvelous coolness of night closed in on him.

Somewhere between half-sleep and sleep, a man came by and introduced himself. A proper introduction would have been, "I am Guy, the deserter," but Guy was too clever a deserter for that. He classified John Vianney immediately: a simple peasant, called to be a soldier, who *really* had lost his regiment, and *really* couldn't find it.

Guy explained the hopelessness of trying to find the lost regiment. It was impossible. John believed him. The case was quite clear in his mind. The will of God had taken another course. God had changed His mind; that was all.

Guy explained the State's unfriendly attitude toward deserters. He was even nice enough to explain what deserters were. The two friends made their way to the nearby town of Les Robins. Mayor Fayot was a good man, known and loved for his big heart. He was well aware of the penalty for desertion but could not refuse the clumsy boy from Dardilly.

"My extra rooms are already filled with two boys such as yourself," the Mayor said kindly. "But you will be safe with my cousin, Claude Fayot." The Fayots liked John, everyone did. He slept in their hayloft, ate at their table, tutored their children and in his spare time studied, painstakingly, his musty Latin books. Two years passed by, slipped amazingly by.

In March, 1810, amnesty was granted to all defaulters. John returned home.

※

His parents were overjoyed to see him again. But they would have a happier day than this, in the distant, hazy future, when they would witness their boy's transformation into a priest of God. Marie Vianney would watch the event from Heaven. She was very sick, even now and lived only a few weeks after he arrived back home.

"John," she smiled, as he gently stroked her forehead, "I will ask God to have Father

Balley accept you back . . . I will ask Him that, John." And she smiled a long and contented smile.

"You look as if your prayer is already answered," he replied.

"Faith, son, you must have faith," she said gently.

"You have faith, don't you, Mother?"

Tears were creeping into his eyes. "Then, have faith that I can learn that impossible Latin."

She only patted his hand and smiled.

✽

Death came to her quietly, almost gently. At last her earthly bonds were broken, and she was free, wonderfully free, to do her work from Heaven.

Chapter 5

AHEAD... ALWAYS AHEAD

Father Balley was jubilant to have his pupil back. John Vianney was even more jubilant to be back. He lived now with the holy pastor and was the object of many hours of private tutoring. The boy attended regular classes at the Presbytery school besides. He was by far the oldest in the class, and the butt of every joke, especially in the philosophy class. John knew they were laughing at him, but he pretended not to notice, and after a while, it didn't hurt a bit. In fact, he even laughed a little himself.

He was now ready for the Minor Seminary at Verriéres. Father Balley was sure of this. The one year course went along well. John was no sensation. He plodded on "humbly and doggedly" and was soon ready for the Major Seminary at Lyons.

Life at the Major Seminary was much different than Ecully or Verriéres. In fact, all the classes were conducted in Latin. John was treated with kindness and much consideration but his head seemed unpenetrable in the matter of Latin. He tried to grasp the difficult studies, which would have challenged the keenest of minds, yet no visible improvement could be wrung from his work. After six months they were forced to send him home. But for him, home was now Ecully; it meant back to Father Balley.

A lonely lad, with hands in pockets, presented himself at the good priest's doorstep. He sat down, and in halted phrases, confused and bewildered, he told the story of failure and discouragement.

"I've decided to become a brother," John said almost with determination.

"You will *not* become a brother," Father Balley said with a firmness which startled the boy. "You will not become a brother," he repeated again. "You will become a priest!"

John became the object of Father Balley's private coaching—hours and hours, day after day, and then he was presented as a candidate for Minor Orders.

❖

The examiners watched the boy who stood before them. He glanced at each of them and panic raced through his body. The only reason why they considered him at all was due to their respect for Father Balley. They asked him questions; the answers he knew, but he only stammered and repeated useless phrases. It was not much of an impression that he made. And he was not accepted.

"I've decided to become a brother,"
John said almost with determination.

Chapter 6

THE BACKBONE OF SOMEONE ELSE

Father Balley was like a rubber punching bag—the harder the blow, the more he bounced right back into action. One can only imagine the state that John Vianney was in by now. He really needed a friend at this most trying time in his life, and Father Balley proved in every way to be a friend.

He happened to know one of the examiners, a man named Father Bochard, very well and went to see him. Father Bochard agreed to a private interview with the slowest lad in France. John was not so afraid to meet just one examiner. In fact, the meeting was quite satisfactory.

❊

Now it remained for John to be accepted by the Cardinal, who happened to be out of town. Bishop Courbon, the diocesan Vicar General, ruled the diocese during the Archbishop's absence.

Bishop Courbon, a short, plump man, had that wonderful gift of making you feel that you were the sole object of his attention. He looked at the tall, slender, eager young man before him. He thought of all the parishes left vacant by the wretched persecution, and then looked back at the boy again.

Turning to Father Balley, he asked, "Is John Vianney good?"

"He is a model of goodness," Father Balley assured him.

"Very well," the simple man said without hesitation, "then let him be ordained. The grace of God will do the rest."

On July 2, 1814, John received Minor Orders. In June, 1815, he was made a deacon.

❋

Deacon Vianney walked sixty miles from the Lyons Seminary to the city of Grenoble. He walked the dusty, dry roads alone. But he was not alone. His mind was preoccupied with only one thought. His heart was singing a wonderful tune. It was still pitch dark when he had begun the journey, but now the sun's first streaks began to appear. This was the morning of the third day. The journey was a long one for a man on foot. But this was the final hurdle of a much longer journey, and at last it was at an end. He reached the Church of the

Minims on August 13, 1815. Here, in this church, on this very day, John Vianney was to be ordained a priest.

When someone commented that the church preparation and ceremonies were all just for one boy, and he not from their diocese at that, the Bishop looked at the dusty, smiling lad who stood before him and said,

"It is never too much trouble to ordain a good priest."

When he went to bed that night, John fell asleep as a priest of God. The mirage had really come true. It didn't seem possible, yet. But the impact would strike, when, in the morning he would offer his first Mass.

Then it was back to Ecully... back to Father Balley.

He looked at the tall, slender, eager young man before him.

Chapter 7

DEATH OF A FRIEND

All of Ecully anxiously awaited the return of the boy who had long ago stolen their hearts.

"Father John, Father John," they shouted as families ran from their houses to greet him. They kissed his consecrated hands and excitedly patted and poked him. He was their boy, the object of so many prayers and they shared in the joy of the victory as well.

John tried to pull away as fast as he could. There was someone else he had to see. The old parish church was now in view, and the drab little house of Father Balley. John knocked nervously on the rectory door. The door quickly opened. Two priests stood looking at one another.

"Come in, Father John," the pastor said warmly. And there were tears on both sides.

✦

Ecully was destined to be the first assignment for Father Vianney. He became curate to the man responsible for his ordination, and Father Balley continued to teach him theology. As yet, Father John still had not been granted the faculty to hear confessions. Meanwhile, the young curate was besieged from all sides. His average sermons caused the church to be filled; countless souls sought his opinion even about the most secret problems. It seemed that the simple people identified themselves with him. Yes, he understood them.

Father Vianney was obviously ready to hear confessions. Father Balley assured the Archbishop that his young curate knew enough moral theology to solve even the most delicate situations, though not necessarily from books. Another victory for the new priest. His confessional was instantly swarmed with penitents, and the first to kneel at his feet was his own pastor.

The two men agreed totally in everything. There was not an ounce of jealousy in the now aging Father Balley at the witnessing of his curate's popularity. In only one thing was there rivalry: the apparent race to outstrip each other in physical mortifications. Father Balley accused his curate of "excess" in this regard, and Father Vianney was quick to return the compliment.

Three years passed by, the happiest years of Father John's young life. And then the saintly Father Balley became very sick and lay dying.

"Here, my poor Vianney," the old man said, handing over to John his instruments of penance.

"Hide them. If people found them after my death, they would believe that I had committed sins which demanded such means of expiation, and so they would leave me in Purgatory until the end of the world."

※

Father John buried his friend's body in a plain little graveyard in that country town of Ecully. But the spirit of Father Balley, now so gloriously radiant in Heaven, followed his beloved Vianney to his next assignment. Sweet memories flooded John's mind of a man, a good man, whom he could never forget. His thoughts were of Father Balley as he trekked the road to Ars.

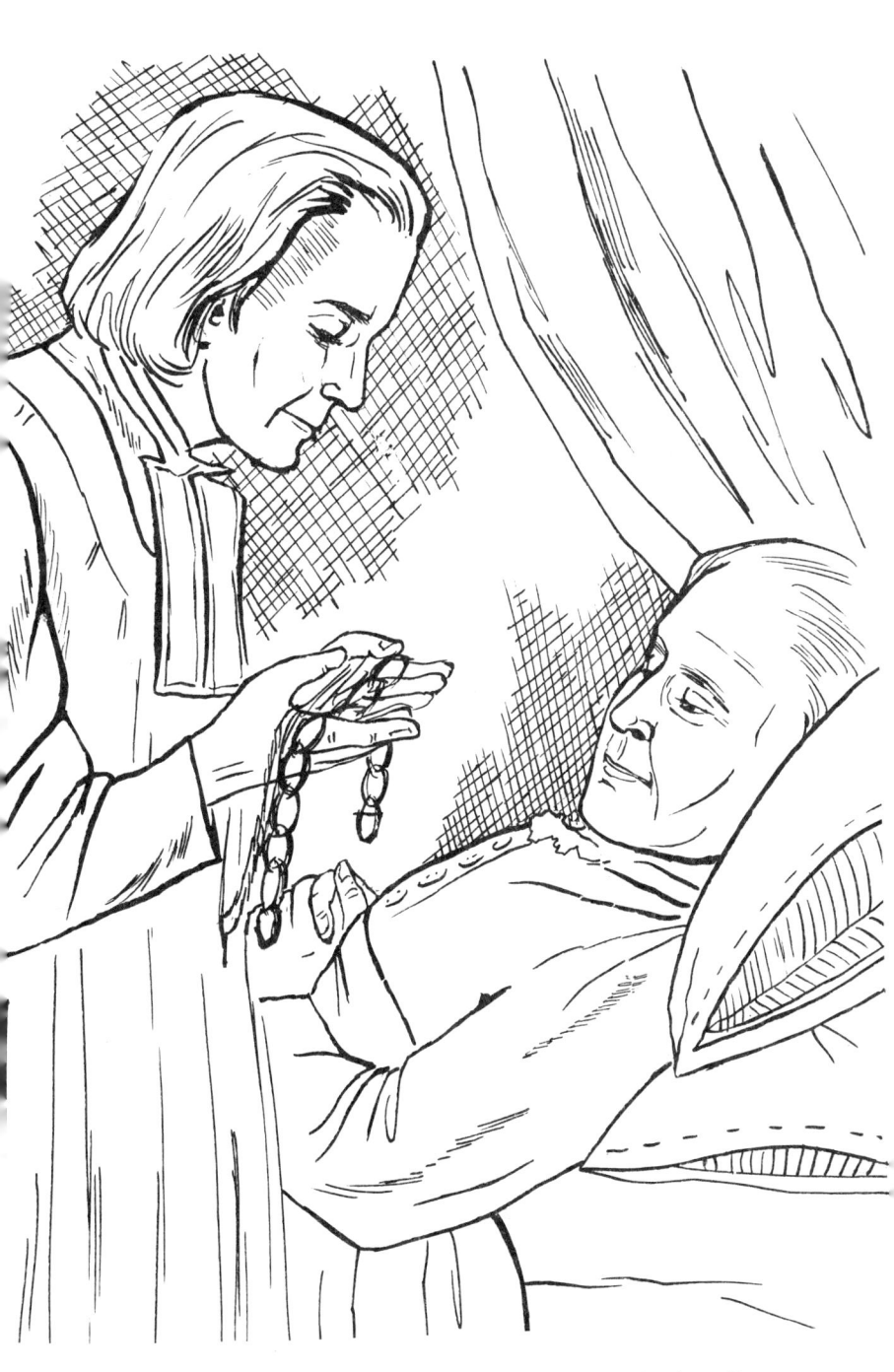

"Here, my poor Vianney," the old man said, "Hide them."

PART II

*"You have not chosen me,
but I have chosen you, and have appointed you
that you should go and bear fruit,
and that your fruit should remain."*
John 15:16

CHAPTER 1

PASTOR OF WHAT?

It was evening, as the lonely figure appeared on the hill which overlooked Ars. The plush green orchards, which had been so much a part of living, had long ago faded into obscurity. Maybe it was the time of day, maybe it was just his mood, but to Father Vianney, everything looked very grey. There were only two streets to this curious town. Drab yellow clay houses lined them. The parallel streets met at the end and there, built a little higher than the rest, was the parish church. Next to it was the empty rectory. Both were badly in need of repairs.

No one was there to meet him. Probably no one knew he was coming. It didn't matter. Life consisted in much more than that. He knelt down on the damp ground of that hill overlooking the town, and prayed for courage, for wisdom and for success in this new endeavor. The parish was small, two hundred and thirty souls in all, but as he knelt there, he found himself saying aloud,

"This parish will not be able to hold all those who later will come to it."

*

He walked slowly down the main street as the last streaks of day were sliding into night. Not a soul was outside, but two hundred thirty pairs of eyes were on that tall, lanky figure, walking toward the church. They watched him from windows, behind cracks in doors, and from haylofts. Father Vianney was the last person in the world to notice it. He walked through the entrance of the barn-like church and stood repulsed at the careless poverty which surrounded his God.

"We'll have to fix it up," he said, partly to Our Lord, partly to himself. He knelt there for a while and then went next door to the rectory. Today that rectory would have had a "Condemned" sign, but then there were no State inspectors. Strangely enough, he liked it just fine.

"It's worthy of me," he smiled to himself.

The six high-back leather chairs, which adorned the otherwise barren parlor, were much too luxurious. Back they went the next morning to the kindly lady who lived in the large red brick manor on the edge of town. She had donated them to his predecessor and assured this strange priest, who stood before her, that he was quite welcome to them too.

"No, I'm just a peasant," he said softly. "Peasants aren't used to things like this." Mille Garnier, known to the town people as the "lady of the Manor," liked him. She liked him instantly.

Chapter 2

ONE MAN ATTACK

As the Curé celebrated Mass on his first morning there, each time that he turned and intoned the "Dominus Vobiscum," a startling pain ripped his heart. Pew after pew was empty. Only a few old ladies were there.

The words of the Vicar General rang in his ears, again and again: "My friend, you have been appointed Curé of Ars. It is a little parish, where there is not much love of God; you must put some into it."

The task grew in immensity as the Curé glanced at the empty church.

❄

Someone described Ars as "in every sense of the word, a hole." It had suffered the effects of distance and the Revolution as well. It wasn't that the people despised religion or even thought themselves enemies of it. They believed in God, but their belief was not solid enough to spill over into everyday life. In fact, they lived from day to day, not really thinking much about it. Sunday was just another day, although many of the women still attended Mass, and even a few men, when it was convenient.

The majority of Ars liked to drink, to dance, to swear. Ignorance in spiritual things was everywhere. Most priests would probably have resigned themselves to maintaining this standard of mediocrity, while fighting to keep the climate from degenerating into something still lower. But Father Vianney had big plans for Ars and the will power to carry them out.

"Now I must begin," he said to himself, as he faced that empty church. "Now I must begin."

He initiated weekly Catechism classes for adults, as well as children, and taught them himself.

❁

Long hours the Curé spent in the stuffy confessional, waiting for people to come. And many an hour nobody came. But there were other ways to win the hearts and weak wills of his parishioners. The physical penances he had begun as a curate to Father Balley, were not only increased, but doubled. He ate almost nothing except one boiled potato for lunch and another for supper. His hours of sleep were cut to minimum and long prayer vigils passed the rest of the night. He scourged his back until the welts opened and the blood oozed out. Were these methods too extreme? No, not when measured with the results which Father Vianney expected. He wanted something for each of his two hundred thirty souls. He wanted one thing for them, *sanctity*. If they did not think enough of his goal to earn it themselves, then he would do enough penance for all of them.

Religious indifference is one enemy which is very hard to fight. It's like trying to get a response from a department store manikin or shouting at someone who is totally deaf.

The Curé's personal visits, and above all, his personal interest, increased the membership at Sunday Mass. When the tall, serious priest turned for the "Dominus Vobiscum," most of the pews weren't empty now. Results were trickling in.

Strong sermons were the next form of attack. Carefully prepared, rehearsed to perfection, they conveyed a definite message, geared to penetrate even the most indifferent soul. His words were practical. They bounced from the pulpit and pierced the ears of the listeners. Sermons on loose dancing, on evil talk (and he quoted the bad language to make sure

He ate almost nothing except one boiled
potato for lunch and another for supper.

they understood just what he meant); sermons on drunkenness (there were seven taverns in that little town); sermons on Sunday rest, on penance and prayer...and sermons on Hell.

"Did the Curé of Ars preach long sermons?" asked a Monsignor who heard him. "Yes," he said, answering his own question. "Long ones, and always on Hell. Ah, well, he believed in it."

❊

Eventually, the two bars closest to the church, closed...not enough business...then two more...the result of much prayer and awesome penances. Why, the townsfolk were even beginning to whisper that their Curé was a saint.

CHAPTER 3

THE PETITION

The Curé was restless. He paced the floor thinking of new ways... new ways of bringing his flock back to Christ. There were a thousand jobs to be done and none of yesterday's victories eased the desires of his heart.

The problem of Sunday rest was working out though. It was obvious that something would have to fill the void in the lives of his families, who had previously harvested their crop on that day. Father Vianney explained the beautiful custom of "Vespers" and taught the correct way to sing them. There followed a rosary and sermon. And a new meaning of Sunday flooded the parish.

But when one battle was won, ten new problems seemed to raise their ominous heads. The outdoor, all-night dancing festivals were one such thorn. They bred impurity and loose living which stood at the extreme opposite of everything which John Vianney believed. He took the matter to the pulpit. There was a good chance that he would make a few enemies, but that always happens when one tries to pit God against the devil. The young girls of the parish were touched to the quick by the earnestness of their Pastor. They were ashamed, and told him so.

"But you are so strict, Father," some would whine.

"I have to be," he would say, pausing for a moment, "because hell is *real*, you know."

All coming festival plans dwindled into nothing, except once, when seven or eight rebellious lads arranged for a festival, despite the wishes of Father Vianney. But the good Curé outwitted them. He met the scheduled violinist, paid him double, and sent him away. Now, what's a dance without music? The whole thing fell through and the boys were furious.

When night fell, they marched in front of the rectory, shouting insults to the "enemy" within, using terrible language, painting his doorstep with the miserable words which fell from their lips.

Father Vianney was in his room, scourging his tortured back for the poor sinners who protested underneath his window. He would

Father Vianney scourged his tortured back for
the poor sinner who protested underneath his window.

beat himself until they went away. They kept it up for hours.

※

Even though the men were now going to Sunday Mass, very few received Holy Communion. It could only be that they did not understand who awaited them at the altar rail.

"It is my duty to make them understand," the Curé thought aloud.

He founded the Confraternity of the Most Holy Sacrament for them and then plunged into membership campaigns. For the women, the Confraternity of the Rosary began. The pious prayers of these good ladies were needed to support the energy-packed endeavors of their pastor.

But there was still more to be done. The Church needed remodeling badly. It didn't matter that the rectory was far worse. It didn't matter at all. The wooden steeple was replaced by a red brick tower. Side chapels were built in, and dedicated to the Saints who were so much a part of the pastor's life. First, a chapel to Mary; another to John the Baptist. When the Curé found himself short of funds with the carpenter pressing for payment, an offering for the exact amount was delivered to Vianney by an anonymous benefactor.

"Faith," he said with tear-filled eyes. "Life requires a lot of Faith."

Pictures and statues of his favorite people decorated the little church: St. Joseph, St. Peter, St. Sixtus, St. Blaise, St. Michael the Archangel, St. Francis of Assisi, St. Benedict Labre and above all, a little obscure first century martyr who struck a marvelous friendship with a straight-laced nineteenth century Curé. He knew her by the name of Philomena. What her name really is, matters little. A chapel was added in her honor, and often her lonely friend would find his way into her quiet nook and talk to her. The graces he asked, she always brought, and the very peace of heaven too. When he called her by name, when he whispered "Philomena," in the silence of his soul, the little martyr knew who he meant, and immediately touched his soul with her presence.

❄

Two more chapels, one to the Ecce Homo and another to the Holy Angels were added. The quiet beauty of this remodeled Church, attracted the people of Ars. Most, even the men, now considered it part of their daily routine, to stop in Church for a visit. They left their farm tools outside the door, and picked them up a short while later, renewed in spirit, ready to continue the day's work.

Now, only the vestments and altar supplies did not meet the approval of the Curé, whose name was becoming synonymous with "perfection". Everything so near his God must be beautiful. The vestments which Father Vianney wore to mount the altar of God were gorgeous enough for any Bishop. And so it should be when a man calls God down to a human altar.

For Vianney the priest, the clothes were the best. For Vianney the man, the wardrobe was unbelievable: one cassock, one pair of heavy peasant shoe-boots, one pair of trousers, one shirt, and a bulky felt hat, which lost it's crown ages ago. But that was plenty for the *man*, Vianney. This remarkable man asked for nothing for himself. He only gave ... everything ... totally. Ars was really a transformed little place. The taverns had long since disappeared. Sunday was now recognized for what it was. The loose festivals were no more. The church, enlarged and remodeled, was always filled for Sunday Mass, and the Communion rail flooded. All of his wildest dreams were coming true. Now, could he rest? Now, could he relax his hours of prayer and inhuman penances? Oh no, life would never be easy for John Vianney. He would never let it become easy.

Nor did he expect thanks, nor even recognition. In fact, there were many among his fellow clergy, who misunderstood him, who questioned his methods, who despised this simpleton who appeared at the yearly retreat, wearing his peasant boots.

Once when a petition for his removal passed through the French countryside and was signed by brother priests, Father Vianney added his name to the list and then turned it in to the Bishop.

The Bishop was quite aware of the criticism which was circulating. He knew the Curé in question and overlooked these foolish things. But when the adjective "mad", was applied to the poor man, Bishop Devie brought the matter up at the annual retreat:

"Gentlemen, I wish that all my clergy had a small grain of the same madness."

Chapter 4

MATES — CURÉ AND THE DEVIL

Spiritual victories, more than the Curé dared hope for, were pouring into his lap. But he suffered plenty for them. Half-starved, beaten and cut, praying for hours, cramming into one day a three day schedule—wasn't this enough to pay for the conversion of a town? Evidently not....

The Curé of Ars climbed up to his second floor bedroom at nine o'clock each night. He slept until one o'clock A.M. — four hours, and then began the new day. Giving up the extra sleep was by far the most difficult sacrifice, but he needed all the hours possible for God.

One night, as the exhausted man just began to relax in bed, he heard the distinct sound of rats scratching the bed posts. He leaped to the floor, grabbed a broom in an attempt to scare the pests away. When he looked, there were no rats at all, nor any claw marks evident. Night after night the clawing continued.

Then toward winter, loud knocks thundered against the bolted back door. Once the Curé bounded down the stairs and threw open the door. But no one was there. And then... the horrible realization. Although there were at least three inches of snow on the ground, no footprints, not one, could be found.

It had to be something from... from another place. Was it the devil? Yes, Father Vianney now understood that it was he, with new tricks to become instruments of torture. There was no visible creature near his bed and yet the Curé would receive slaps hard enough to knock him to the floor. The furnishings in his meager room would fly through the air and crash against the walls. There would be piercing screams—endless and filled with hell's misery. Why was the devil forced to such extreme measures? Because this poor country priest had become so much in command of himself that ordinary temptations proved futile.

When a person limits his repose to four hours a night, he needs every bit of it to be sound sleep. Now if the devil kept a man awake for that time, obviously he would break him. Evidently, that was what the devil thought. There were so many different ways to keep the man from sleep. The sound of horses thundering through the house, the steady noise of dripping water, eerie music, the tapping of invisible finger tips on a table top, a flock of bats hovering over his bed, or a snarling black dog with flashing red eyes—they were all the same person. They were all the devil. At first Father Vianney lay in bed with teeth chattering loudly. Then as the days turned into weeks and the weeks into years, he almost grew used to it.

"We're mates: the devil and I," he would smile in his good-natured way.

From 1824 to 1858, hell followed Vianney in the most harsh and extreme of ways, with every coy and clever manifestation possible, but the devil never won. After thirty-five years, he gave up—the external manifestations at least.

CHAPTER 5

ARS GROWS

It was too good to be true—the life of this remarkable man, that is. Ars could not hide him for themselves. His reputation for sanctity had oozed out of that little hamlet and was gliding across the French countryside.

In 1827, the first pilgrims began to trickle in. Some came to see the man who alone had reformed an entire town. Others came to catch a glimpse of one who struggled physically with the devil. Some came, most came, to seek this gentle man in the quiet of the confessional, this man whom they knew would understand, and they unburdened the guilt of years and years.

From 1830 until 1845, over three hundred visitors came daily to see him, to ask his help.

"Do you know why all these people crowd your little church?" one of his close friends asked him.

"Yes," he smiled. "They have come to see the chapel of my little Philomena, to venerate her relics."

"Oh no," the man insisted, "Crowds this large have not come to venerate a dead saint, but a living one...."

✦

Pilgrims brought more pilgrims. In fact, the powerful railroad came to Ars. Eight-day round trips were scheduled from Lyons for the eager masses of humanity who flocked to see him. They *had* to allow eight days for no one could expect to see the Curé in less than that.

His daily schedule became something like this:

1:00 A.M. (In the morning) He said his prayers in church. Until 6:00 A.M. he heard confessions of women.

6:00 He said Mass and made his Thanksgiving until 8:00 A.M. He was at the service of the faithful, to bless images or give advice.

8:00 Breakfast at Convent of La Providence just across the square. (Breakfast was ½ glass of milk without any thing else.)

8:30 Confessions of men in sacristy.

10:00 Little Hours of the Office, then more Confessions until 11:00 A.M.
11:00 Catechism class for children and grown ups.
12:00 Noon. Angelus—then lunch
12:30 P.M. Visits to the parish sick (always with a crowd following).
2:00 Vespers and Compline; women's confessions until 5:00 P.M.
5:00 to 8:00 Confessions of men.
8:00 Evening prayers and Rosary; finished Office.
Between 9:00 and 10:00 Supper (one boiled potato—the week's supply kept on stove in pot of water) then bed until 1:00 A.M.

However, as the crowds grew, he would occasionally hear confessions from 10:00 until Midnight. Then one hour of sleep, and his new day began *on schedule,* at 1:00 A.M.

There were no physical chains which bound Father Vianney to his unbelievable task. But day after patterned day, he was there, whether he was sick or not, whether he was rested or not, whether he felt like it or not. Always he was working for Christ and it took the patience of a saint.

The crowd was always present. The devil taunted his private moments of repose. Miracles were happening at the touch of his hand, which embarrassed him beyond words. His physical condition was so bad that doctors agreed it was only a miracle which kept him alive. And always the people waited, sometimes for days on end, for him.

But life was beautiful for John Vianney, because twenty hours of every day he was acting as God's priest, bringing His Son to poor, starving men.

Chapter 6

CHAMBER OF MERCY

People were coming from hundreds of miles away. They came to find a man who had become a legend, while still alive. They came to the now famous Ars, without an invitation, without an appointment, but never even doubting their chances of seeing Father Vianney. He had time for everyone if they could just wait long enough. Many waited in line for twelve hours and more, going without food and water. And if their turn never came, bright and early the next morning, they returned.

When a man knelt to confess to the Curé, he felt brave and capable of confessing even the most humiliating sins with accuracy and honesty. The words came so spontaneously... and sorrow, real sorrow, flooded the soul. And then hope, courage, optimism, followed. The words of the good Father Vianney filled the now peaceful soul in front of him. He would say only a sentence—maybe two—of advice, but it was practical, sensible and would last a lifetime.

A few sought the Curé out of curiosity and returned from necessity. Some tried to hide the state of their soul or to conceal a sin, and then he would tell them what was missing.

❊

Eleven hours a day, he spent in the confessional. In the winter his toes became numb with cold and his fingers could scarcely feel the rosary beads that he held. In the summer, the sultry humidity closed in on the little church, till the very walls were drenched. Still the Curé was at his post, adjusting to any and all of the elements; a priest he would be in all kinds of weather.

The crowds grew steadily larger. Now it was obvious, even to Father Vianney, that they were here to see him, to hear his words of absolution of their souls. By cutting corners on his sleep and intensifying his daily schedule, he was now available for confession, sixteen to seventeen hours every day.

Sometimes he would weep at the tale of offenses against God, and after each sin would cry,

"What a pity! What a pity!"

To an Archbishop, who knelt for absolution, the Curé gave only one line of admonition:

"Love your clergy very much."

To the Superior General of a Teaching Institute, he said,

"Love the good God very much."

But those words—backed by a life of prayer and mortification, like the gold which gives value to paper money—those words took root and bore fruit, for it was Christ the Priest who spoke.

The prayers of Vianney followed each person as he left the church and walked out into the light of ordinary living. He never forgot a soul. He often forgot supper, or what the weather was like, or the critical remark of a careless tongue, but he never forgot a soul.

In that miserable prison-like confessional Father Vianney was happy, for soul after soul found God again or became more closely united to Him, and in a strange and wonderful way he, the Curé of Ars, helped to bring it about.

The 11:00 A.M. instruction, which once had been held at the orphanage, was now moved to the church. Even the church bulged to the very seams.

It was touching to see the aging priest, with striking white hair, mount the pulpit and look out over the crowd with such love. They were spell-bound just by his presence. Age had mellowed him. The long, fiery sermons on hell were no more. Now he talked on love of God and neighbor. Tears lit his eyes as he explained the malice of sin and the hurt it causes the good God. Nor were these the senile tears of an old man. The entire flock cried right with him.... There were countless clergymen, far more learned than he, who sat with tears streaming. The Curé of Ars understood *who* God was, *what* sin is—and best of all, he knew how to make others understand too.

Bishops, priests, religious, rich, poor, learned, simple, good, bad, lay, cleric found peace at that dumpy little town, called Ars, because a saint made his home there.

Eleven hours a day he spent in the confessional.

Chapter 7

LOOKING IN – OR THROUGH
– A SOUL

The Baroness de Lacomble waited in the stuffy country church, despairing of ever getting so much as one word with the Curé. Suddenly the wizard-like man emerged from his confessional hermitage, and walked straight toward her.

"Let them marry. They will be very happy," he whispered.

The Baroness' mouth dropped open... that was the very answer to the problem on which she had so much desired his opinion. Her eighteen year old son was about to marry a fifteen year old girl. Would they be happy? That was all this mother sought—her child's happiness. Now everything was all right. Father Vianney had said they would be happy and it would be so.

❈

One grey afternoon, Father Vianney stopped a strange girl:

"Is it you who have written to me, my child?"

"Yes, Father."

"Very well. You must not worry. You will enter the convent, all right. The Reverend Mother will contact you in a few days," and it was so.

❂

The countless miracles of physical healing he attributed to his lovely Philomena. But not everyone believed it was she. In fact, it was kind of hard to understand his tributes to her, when it was the touch of his hand which made the hideous tumor on a child's face fade into nothingness.

❂

His clothes were thread-bare, his white hair unkempt, and face thin and drawn, but for all of his foibles and unusual appearance, he was in every sense of the word, a priest. One could have dressed him in a clown suit and marched him in a parade, but still could have pointed him out for what he was—a priest. It showed clear through, both inside and out.

Chapter 8

A MONK AT HEART

Souls for Christ—that was his chief concern. But, he who was so interested in saving others, was he going to save himself?

The devil's famous last visible stand was really quite final. People were running into church and causing a commotion. The Curé poked his head from the confessional.

"There are flames coming from your room!" they shouted. He gave them the house key, so that they could put out the fire. And then with a sigh, he said,

"This wretched fiend—he has not been able to catch the bird, so he has burnt the cage." That, in fact, was the exact situation. The devil had caused the Curé's bed to burst into flames.

"Now I am truly the poorest man in this town," Father Vianney mused, "for the poor all have a bed to sleep in, but I don't even have that." And he could honestly say he was glad.

❁

The devil had exhausted all of his tricks, and after thirty-five years it seemed he would admit defeat. But that was only from a superficial view. His approach would now of necessity be different.

"I am so interested in saving others," the Curé thought. "My own prayers are cut to a very minimum. The crowd is always around me. Am I saving them and neglecting my own soul? Fool . . . fool . . . fool. Some quiet corner of a monastery—that's all I ask. To be alone with God, to make ready my soul to meet Him. I must leave Ars and prepare to die."

❁

Of course he would leave by night. He did not go out the front door, but climbed over the hedge at the back. The ever alert crowd saw him and rushed after the lean, white-haired priest, who was definitely up to mischief. He did leave Ars. Seven hours later, he reentered the house of his youth. The Bishop sent a message there, assuring Father Vianney that he was not allowed to accept a parish outside of the diocese.

But what would the good Bishop say if he knew that his famous Curé was really seeking the silence of a cloister?

Father Vianney left on Thursday. On Friday, a large crowd of pilgrims besieged the house, begging him to come out and hear their confessions.

On Saturday, a deputation of twenty-three young men came from Ars representing the whole parish. They wanted Father Vianney and no other back.

At last the poor man began to weep.

"God does not want me here. Let us get back to Ars."

❊

As the suffering travelers from all over France crowded to that Ars confessional, the Curé said in all simplicity,

"What would have become of so many poor sinners?"

❊

Ten years later the desire for the monastery proved too strong again.

"You cannot leave without your breviary," his assistant, Father Toccanier, said to him as he grabbed it out of the Curé's hand.

"Give it back!" the Curé exclaimed.

"No," was the firm reply.

"I have another one at home," the Curé declared. "I will get it."

He stepped out into the courtyard. The ever-waiting crowd, knowing of his plans to leave, thrust themselves at him.

"You cannot leave without your breviary,"
his assistant, Father Toccanier said to him as
he grabbed it out of the Cure's hand.

"Hear my confession . . . and mine . . . and mine." They clutched at the old priest, tearing pieces of material from his cassock.

"What misguided devotion," he muttered.

All the while, Father Toccanier taunted him from behind,

"You who love the saints so much, why is it that you forget the example of St. Martin, who said, 'I do not refuse work.' Or what about St. Philip Neri, who said that even if he were on the threshold of heaven, he would willingly turn his back on it to hear the confession of a sinner?"

The Saints—how the Curé loved the Saints. Were they beckoning to him now? Yes, at last it was all so clear. Ars was his home until death. His work was the prayer that God wanted of him. Each of those miserable sinners was Christ and he, Vianney, the priest, must continue to help make them whole.

The quiet perfection of a stone-walled monastery would never be known to Father Vianney. But the desire for contemplation was not to be extinguished. His road to heaven passed through Ars. He was to spend his life as a simple parish priest, not a monk. This was God's will, and now the Curé knew it. But the remarkable fact of it all is this—every one of his years at Ars was spent there against his own will.

Chapter 9

THE ETERNAL PILGRIMAGE

He was always dying, yet he did not die. At the end men had come to believe that he would never die.

How did he look in those last years of his life? An eye-witness said that his body gave the impression of a "shade"—in truth one saw through it, and the soul, burning in the great sunken eyes, shone through the transparent yellow of his face and hands.

In spite of the continual cross of sickness, old age, the milling crowds, the torture of sleepless days and nights, the stifling heat of summer and the damp cold of winter, and a list of added tortures, known only to this gentle man, he continued to spend sixteen to seventeen hours a day in the confessional.

"I've made up my mind," he said. "I will die working. If God refused my offer to live a contemplative life, then, I will die working."

Only the doctors knew how sick he really was. Yet, more and more frequently Father Vianney was mentioning the expectation of death.

✽

It was 1859. Over one hundred thousand pilgrims had come to Ars that year. Those who packed the courtyard on July 29, had courage and patience—a lot of both, for the heat had reached staggering proportions.

On the way to church, the Curé fainted and fell on the stairs, leading from his room. Luckily no one saw and he continued his day's schedule, as usual.

When he returned to his room that night, the Curé sank into the nearest chair and murmured—still with that wonderful optimism—

"I can do no more. Sinners will kill the sinner...."

They put him to bed and when Father Toccanier, his assistant, came to the room, the Curé was ice cold and horribly white.

At 1:00, the waiting crowd missed his familiar presence. Nor did he come at 2:00 or 3:00 or 4:00 ... nor would he ever walk into that church again.

In the morning, a mattress was placed under his tortured body, and a Sister from the girl's school hovered over him, touching wet cloths to his face, giving him liquids to drink, and frantically trying to brush the flies away.

"Leave me my poor flies," he said quietly. "Nothing bothers me but sin."

❋

Somehow they knew without anyone telling them; the masses below in the square called up to the poor, dying Curé,

"Hear my confession"; Bless my children"; Pray for me."

For four days in that torrid heat, as the last days of July turned into August, Father Vianney lay dying.

He made his confession, his last confession, and then a group of priests, each bearing a lighted candle, filed in solemn procession to his room. They brought with them the most beautiful gift that Father Vianney could ask for.

For forty-five years, this good priest had gone to the church to bring Christ to the people of Ars. For forty-five years he had visited their homes to bring Christ into their family circle. And now... now when the country priest's body was broken beyond repair, and his soul longed for the promise of heaven, now when he could no longer go to the Master, the Master came to him.

"It is sad to be making one's last Communion," he said softly. And as the Host-Christ was placed on his tongue, tears, silent yet abundant, flowed down his cheeks.

❉

And then he died, silently, serenely. There was "no struggle, no violence, no agony." He just went to sleep on that sultry night in early August and awoke in eternity.

❉

Three hundred priests and thousands of the faithful walked in the funeral procession on that sixth day of August. They were paying final tribute to a man, a good man, just a simple parish priest from the backwoods of Ars.

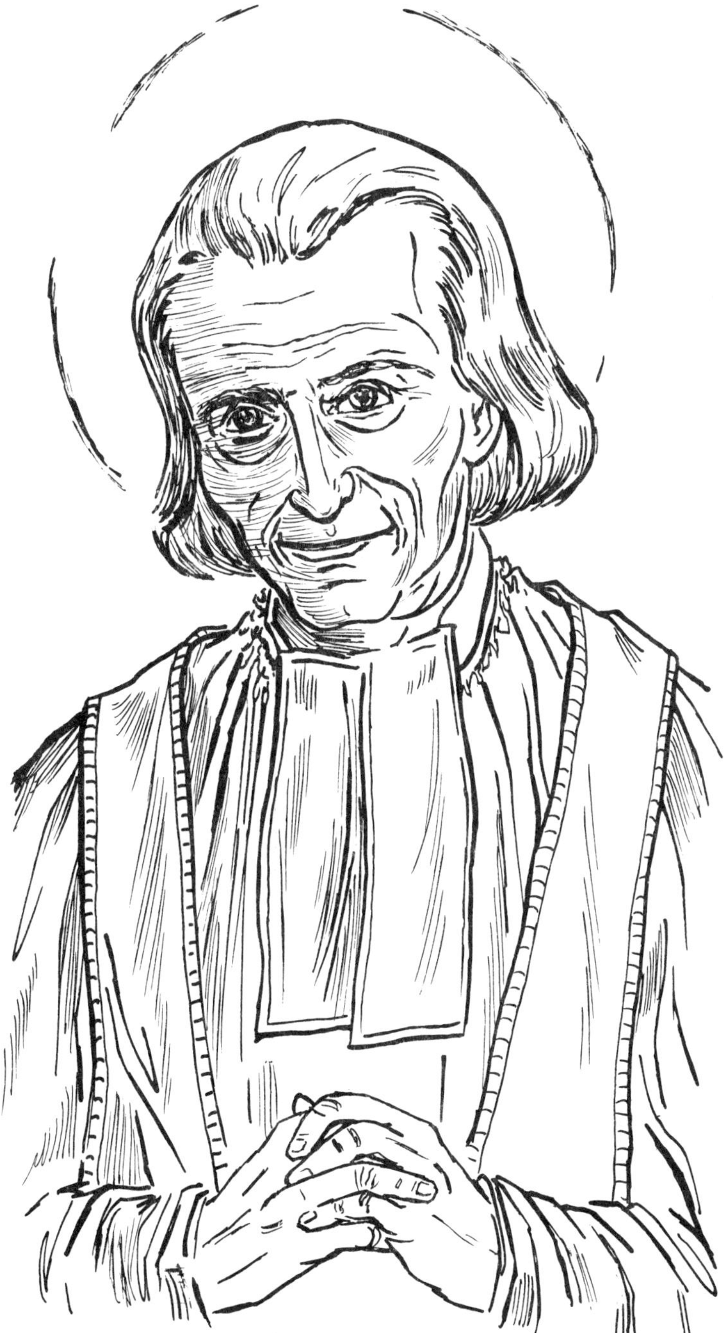

GREAT HEROES OF GOD

DSP Encounter Books

A goldmine of enjoyable reading and wholesome inspiration, written in a smooth-flowing style for fourth to eighth graders (and their families). Great heroes and saints of God come alive with all the dynamism of their noble ideals. Each volume illustrated.

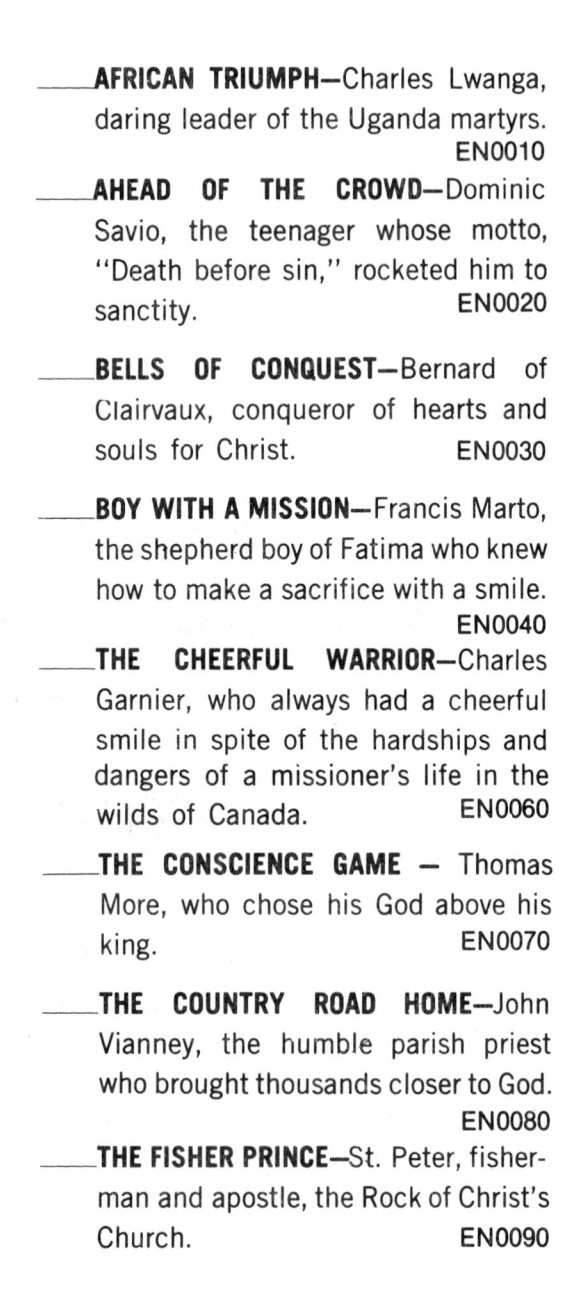

____**AFRICAN TRIUMPH**—Charles Lwanga, daring leader of the Uganda martyrs. EN0010

____**AHEAD OF THE CROWD**—Dominic Savio, the teenager whose motto, "Death before sin," rocketed him to sanctity. EN0020

____**BELLS OF CONQUEST**—Bernard of Clairvaux, conqueror of hearts and souls for Christ. EN0030

____**BOY WITH A MISSION**—Francis Marto, the shepherd boy of Fatima who knew how to make a sacrifice with a smile. EN0040

____**THE CHEERFUL WARRIOR**—Charles Garnier, who always had a cheerful smile in spite of the hardships and dangers of a missioner's life in the wilds of Canada. EN0060

____**THE CONSCIENCE GAME** — Thomas More, who chose his God above his king. EN0070

____**THE COUNTRY ROAD HOME**—John Vianney, the humble parish priest who brought thousands closer to God. EN0080

____**THE FISHER PRINCE**—St. Peter, fisherman and apostle, the Rock of Christ's Church. EN0090

____**FLAME IN THE NIGHT**—Francis Xavier, pioneer missionary to the mysterious Far East. EN0100

____**FOOTSTEPS OF A GIANT**—Charles Borromeo's tireless labor during the Council of Trent continued afterwards in fidelity to reform, to change of heart and conduct in the flock entrusted to him. EN0110

____**GIRL IN THE STABLE**—Germaine, the quiet and gentle girl who never felt sorry for herself. EN0130

____**GOD'S SECRET AGENT**—Father Michael Pro, S.J., a modern martyr and daring hero for Christ. EN0140

____**HER DREAM CAME TRUE**—Imelda, a young girl with an overpowering love for Christ in the Eucharist. EN0160

____**LIGHT IN THE GROTTO**—Bernadette, "the little nobody" who brought the world to our Lady's feet. EN0170

____**LOVE AS STRONG AS DEATH**—St. Thecla, the courageous virgin who followed Christ in spite of trial and torment. EN0180

____**A WOMAN WHO LOVED**—Louise de Marillac—lovely, aristocratic, happy and saintly. EN0190

____**MARY'S PILGRIM**—Peregrine—from a teenage gang leader he became a leader for Christ through a powerful friendship with Mary. EN0200

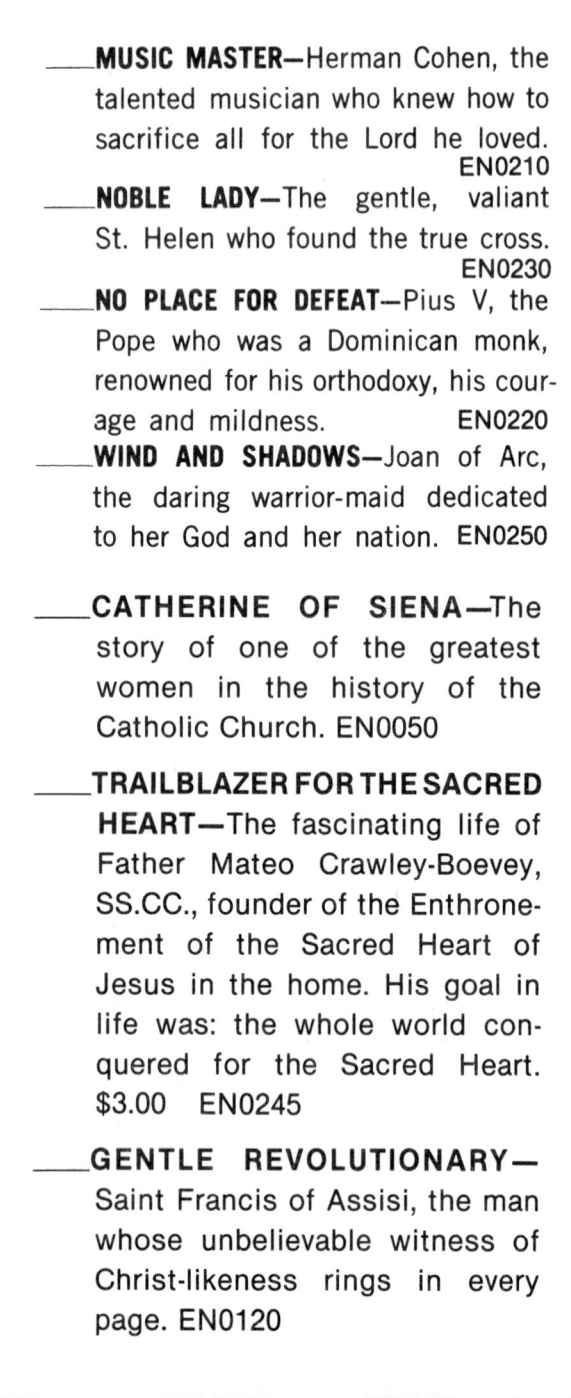

___**MUSIC MASTER**—Herman Cohen, the talented musician who knew how to sacrifice all for the Lord he loved. EN0210

___**NOBLE LADY**—The gentle, valiant St. Helen who found the true cross. EN0230

___**NO PLACE FOR DEFEAT**—Pius V, the Pope who was a Dominican monk, renowned for his orthodoxy, his courage and mildness. EN0220

___**WIND AND SHADOWS**—Joan of Arc, the daring warrior-maid dedicated to her God and her nation. EN0250

___**CATHERINE OF SIENA**—The story of one of the greatest women in the history of the Catholic Church. EN0050

___**TRAILBLAZER FOR THE SACRED HEART**—The fascinating life of Father Mateo Crawley-Boevey, SS.CC., founder of the Enthronement of the Sacred Heart of Jesus in the home. His goal in life was: the whole world conquered for the Sacred Heart. $3.00 EN0245

___**GENTLE REVOLUTIONARY**—Saint Francis of Assisi, the man whose unbelievable witness of Christ-likeness rings in every page. EN0120

___**THE GREAT HERO**—St. Paul the Apostle—adventures of the greatest among the pioneers and saints. EN0150

___**NO GREATER LOVE**—Father Damien, the apostle to Molokai, who gave his life for his lepers. EN0219

___**PILLAR IN THE TWILIGHT***—Thomas Aquinas, the "Dumb Ox" who became a great teacher. EN0240

___**YES IS FOREVER**—Mother Thecla Merlo—the strong, faith-filled co-Foundress of the Daughters of St. Paul. EN0260

___**CAME THE DAWN**—Mary of Nazareth, the Mother of Jesus and ours, too. EN0045

Daughters of St. Paul

MASSACHUSETTS
50 St. Paul's Ave., Jamaica Plain, Boston, MA 02130 **617-522-8911**.
172 Tremont Street, Boston, MA 02111 **617-426-5464; 617-426-4230**.

NEW YORK
78 Fort Place, Staten Island, NY 10301 **718-447-5071; 718-447-5086**.
59 East 43rd Street, New York, NY 10017 **212-986-7580**.
625 East 187th Street, Bronx, NY 10458 **212-584-0440**.
525 Main Street, Buffalo, NY 14203 **716-647-6044**.

NEW JERSEY
Hudson Mall Route 440 and Communipaw Ave.,
 Jersey City, NJ 07304 **201-433-7740**.

CONNECTICUT
202 Fairfield Ave., Bridgeport, CT 06604 **203-335-9913**.

OHIO
2105 Ontario Street (at Prospect Ave.), Cleveland, OH 44115 **216-621-9427**.
616 Walnut Street, Cincinnati, OH 45202 **513-421-5733**.

PENNSYLVANIA
1719 Chestnut Street, Philadelphia, PA 19103 **215-568-2638; 215-864-0991**.

VIRGINIA
1025 King Street, Alexandria, VA 22314 **703-549-3806**.

SOUTH CAROLINA
243 King Street, Charleston, SC 29401 **803-577-0175**.

FLORIDA
2700 Biscayne Blvd., Miami, FL 33137 **305-573-1618**.

LOUISIANA
4403 Veterans Memorial Blvd. Metairie, LA 70006 **504-887-7631; 504-887-0113**.
423 Main Street, Baton Rouge, LA 70802 **504-336-1504; 504-381-9485**.

MISSOURI
1001 Pine Street (at North 10th), St. Louis, MO 63101 **314-621-0346**.

ILLINOIS
172 North Michigan Ave., Chicago, IL 60601 **312-346-4228; 312-346-3240**.

TEXAS
114 Main Plaza, San Antonio, TX 78205 **512-224-8101**.

CALIFORNIA
1570 Fifth Ave. (at Cedar Street), San Diego, CA 92101 **619-232-1442**.
46 Geary Street, San Francisco, CA 94108 **415-781-5180**.

WASHINGTON
2301 Second Ave. (at Bell), Seattle, WA 98121 **206-441-3300**.

HAWAII
1143 Bishop Street, Honolulu, HI 96813 **808-521-2731**.

ALASKA
750 West 5th Ave., Anchorage, AK 99501 **907-272-8183**.

CANADA
3022 Dufferin Street, Toronto 395, Ontario, Canada.

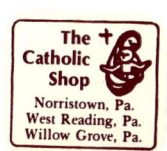

The
Catholic
Shop
Norristown, Pa.
West Reading, Pa.
Willow Grove, Pa.